CITY OF SANDCASTLES

HAGAR PEETERS

CITY OF SANDCASTLES

SELECTED POEMS

TRANSLATED FROM THE DUTCH BY
JUDITH WILKINSON

All rights reserved. No part of this work covered by the copyright herein may be reproduced or used in any means—graphic, electronic, or mechanical, including copying, recording, taping, or information storage and retrieval systems—without written permission of the publisher.

Printed by imprintdigital
Upton Pyne, Exeter
www.digital.imprint.co.uk

Typesetting and cover design by narrator
www.narrator.me.uk
info@narrator.me.uk
033 022 300 39

Published by Shoestring Press
19 Devonshire Avenue, Beeston, Nottingham, NG9 1BS
(0115) 925 1827
www.shoestringpress.co.uk

First published 2018
© Copyright: Judith Wilkinson
© Author photograph: "Hagar Peeters" by Koos Breukel
© Cover image: "Sand-sculpture" by sand-sculptor Sikke-Bart Frieling, www.zandvorm.nl

The moral right of the authors have been asserted.

ISBN 978-1-912524-18-1

This book was published with the support of the Dutch Foundation for Literature

Nederlands letterenfonds
dutch foundation
for literature

ACKNOWLEDGEMENTS

Translations included in this collection, or earlier versions of these translations, have appeared in the following journals: *Acumen, Dutch, Erbacce, The High Window, De Hoffeskrant, Loch Raven Review, The Manhattan Review, Modern Poetry in Translation, Poetry Salzburg Review* and in the anthologies *The Enchanting Verses Literary Review* (India 2017) and *What's Poetry?* (Forum Penyair Internasional Indonesia 2012).

I am grateful to Hagar Peeters for her feedback and suggestions.

I would like to thank my mother, Han Wilkinson-Dekhuijzen, and Anthony Runia for their scrutiny of the translations, and my brother Michael Wilkinson for a few very good finds.

I am greatly indebted to the Dutch Foundation for Literature for providing a translation grant.

Thanks are also due to Hagar Peeters' publisher for permission to publish these translations: Uitgeverij De Bezige Bij. The titles of the original source texts are: *Genoeg Gedicht over de Liefde Vandaag*, Uitgeverij Podium, Amsterdam 1999; *Koffers Zeelucht*, Uitgeverij De Bezige Bij, Amsterdam 2003; *Loper van Licht*, Uitgeverij De Bezige Bij, Amsterdam 2008; *Wasdom*, Uitgeverij De Bezige Bij, Amsterdam 2011 and *Gedichten voor Wich*, Wich & de Vos Foundation, Rotterdam 2012.

CONTENTS

Introduction   1

ENOUGH ABOUT LOVE FOR TODAY

'Shall I Walk with You Some of the Way?'	7
Walking a Tightrope	8
You're No Longer Small Enough	9
I lie waiting in the white	10
The trapeze artist falls.	11
The sea, the sea, the seaaaaaa	12
Date	13
Twoness	14
For years now you've occupied	15

A SUITCASE FULL OF SEA AIR

Last Night I Ran into My Parents	19
A Soft Stone	20
The Same Sea	21
God Help Us That Father of Mine	22
The Diamond	23
She rang the bell. A drawn-out scream	24
The Great Trek	25
Memory of an Unfinished Moment	26
The Sea Is an Eternal Murmurer	27
In Their Shadow	28
A Last Salute	29
If Ever	30
Your Body	31
A Foregone Conclusion	32
Note	33
Illusion	34
Goodbye	35
Holland's Deluge	36
Ecce Homo	37
Lament of the Sleepless Sleeping Beauty	38
Lament of Those Who Listen to War Reports	40

RUNNER OF LIGHT

In the Desert	43
Exile	45
In the Name	46
Ites	49
Reassuring	50
Broken	51
She Knew	52
How I Sounded	53
Miserable	54
The Door Ajar	55
Place of Anticipation	57
What Followed	58
An Example	59
Advice—No Strings Attached	60
En Route	61
Rules of the Game	62
Even the Wind Has an Opinion	63
The Saying Goes	64
Hagar's Ambitions	65

FRUITION

My Grandmother Was a Front Soldier	71
The Grandmother and the Prince	73
God's Flossers	74
Matriarch	75
In the Museum	76
The Vague Rumour	77
Debut	78
After Hans Andreus	79
The One He Was Looking for	80
The Accident	81
I Recognise You	82
For Remco Campert	83
I Caressed Your Poems	84
The Call I Heard in Myself	85
Memento of the Folkingestraat in Groningen	86

Poems for Wich

Boat	89
The Light of the Sea	90
About Décors	92
Décors and in the Meantime	93
Still Life	94
This poem confirms	95
Later I'll be just as old as you were when you went.	96
Notes	98
Biographical Notes	99

INTRODUCTION

Hagar Peeters, born in 1972 in Amsterdam, is one of Holland's most celebrated poets and the recipient of many awards.

Before Peeters had published any poems she was already performing in youth clubs, and her early poems sound like songs, combining lyrical and comic elements. After secondary school she studied Cultural History and Literature at the University of Utrecht. Among the poets she befriended in Utrecht was Ingmar Heytze, who set up a 'poetry circus' where young poets could perform their work. Peeters soon began to be noticed: she was frequently invited to perform at venues and poetry festivals all over the country.

When her first collection appeared in 1999, *Genoeg Gedicht over de Liefde Vandaag* ('Enough about love for today'), it immediately established her as a bold and distinctive new voice. After obtaining a first for her Master's degree, Peeters reworked and extended her thesis, which had won a national award; it was published in 2002 under the title *Gerrit de Stotteraar—Biografie van een Boef* ('Gerrit the Stammerer—biography of a scoundrel'). In it she examines the life of this notorious Dutch burglar and escape artist in the context of the changes in the Dutch criminal justice system in the first decades after the Second World War and she illustrates how the Dutch penal system changed from very mild to the harsh climate of today.

Her subsequent collections—four books and a pamphlet—were well-received too and have seen many reprints. In 2008 she was shortlisted for the position of Poet Laureate. She is also a critic and columnist and has written for several major Dutch newspapers. In addition she has worked as an editor and compiled and introduced numerous anthologies, including a selection of poems by Cavafy, in a Dutch translation, and a selection of poems by the well-known Dutch poet Vasalis.

More recently she has turned to novel-writing and her first novel, *Malva*, based on the life of the illegitimate daughter of Neruda, was published in 2015. The book won the prestigious Flemish Fintro prize. An English translation of *Malva* was published in 2018 in the US by DoppleHouse Press, and a French and a Spanish (South American) edition are also forthcoming.

Peeters has performed her work at many international festivals, such as Poetry International and the Indonesian International Poetry Festival.

She contests that her poems are autobiographical. She feels her work is reflective and analyses human motivation. Sometimes it is necessary to exaggerate: 'I discovered that by magnifying a feeling or a situation I would grasp its essence more easily. By distorting reality you sometimes get closer to reality.'

Much has been written about Peeters' work. Many critics have commented on the sensual nature of her love poetry, where lyricism is tempered by an earthy note. Critic Annette van den Bosch reflects on how Peeters always stays close to everyday reality and is able to shift from laconic to loving to sardonic in her observations.

Aleid Truijens emphasizes how Peeters is a poet who is not afraid of big emotions. Her world is not a pastel-coloured one; it is made up of vibrant tones, unusual imagery and often relies on bizarre mental leaps.

Hans Groenewegen focuses on how Peeters frequently combines everyday language with more formal terms, which sometimes creates a curious kind of tension and even a deliberate 'jarring'. Groenewegen also comments on the 'note of strangeness' and the fairy-tale elements in many of her poems, which contribute to a sense of alienation. In this he detects the influence of two other contemporary poets, Alfred Schaffer and Jan Baeke, whose poems often evoke an atmosphere of displacement.

Poet and critic Arie van den Berg sees echoes of Nijhoff, an early twentieth-century poet who aimed for emotionally charged poems that relied on 'ordinary' language. Van den Berg adds that Peeters' work is more down to earth and less serene than Nijhoff's.

The selection I made for this book was a personal one. Peeters later made some additions, such as the poems inspired by the Dutch poet Remco Campert's work.

In the first section of this book I chose poems from Peeters' first collection, *Genoeg Gedicht over de Liefde Vandaag*, which contains many love poems. I admired their immediacy and the very natural mix of comedy and lyricism, as in the poem 'You're No Longer Small Enough', with its blend of tenderness and witty observation. Already there are more reflective poems too, such as 'Walking a Tightrope' and 'I Lie Waiting in the White'. A strong personality comes through in these poems.

In her next collection, *Koffers Zeelucht* ('A suitcase full of sea air'), an ambitious poet is emerging. I chose a number of poems from the early part of the book that paint a picture of a broken family, seen from the perspective of the daughter. With great economy these grimly ironic poems bring alive the three members of this family, with the speaker's longing filtering through each poem. The book then moves on to an array of different poems, showing a more public poet; in addition to poems about love relationships there are poems that convey broader concerns, such as 'Lament of Those who Listen to War Reports'.

The extraordinary collection *Loper van Licht* ('Runner of light') was loosely inspired by the biblical story of Hagar, the slave who bore Abraham a son and was later banished to the desert. In these poems Hagar, who is never a simple victim, becomes a mouthpiece for all outcasts and outsiders, and Peeters effortlessly darts back and forth between the story of Sarah and Abraham and those of refugees today. I included both the first and the last poem in this collection, namely 'In the Desert' and 'Hagar's Ambitions'. In that final poem—a long literary polemic in which Hagar claims her place in a world still dominated by men—the tirade is characteristically good-humoured, with Hagar mockingly asserting: 'I want to knock around with the great men'.

Peeters' kaleidoscopic collection *Wasdom* ('Fruition') contains poems written in her late teens and early twenties as well as recent work, and Peeters decided not to specify the poems' time of origin. I chose a number of poems from the book's first section, including two powerful portraits of her grandmother that reflect the stifling atmosphere of her Catholic background. To demonstrate the range of Peeters' work, I selected poems on different themes, such as a poem about Groningen's former Jewish quarter and the beautiful 'I Recognise You', with its lyrical evocation of intimacy and its down-to-earth ending.

Peeters' last, short collection, *Gedichten voor Wich* ('Poems for Wich'), celebrating the life of artist and set designer Harry Wich, reveals a quieter voice. In some of the poems I selected, such as

'About Décors', Peeters draws the reader into the magic of the theatre; in other, more understated poems she delicately dwells on the losses Wich suffered and on the passing of time.

I worked on this book intermittently for several years, which gave me time to become intimately familiar with Hagar's oeuvre. I tried to reproduce the effects of the original poems and I followed Peeters' layout, diction, rhymes and half-rhymes as much as possible. I aimed at similar cadences to those of the Dutch, where the rhythms sometimes run counter to expectation and help lend a certain muscularity to the poems.

In the punctuation I again took my cues from the source texts: in some instances Peeters opts for a more fluid effect, with minimal punctuation, especially at the end of lines, at other times she punctuates heavily. As for the order in which I arranged the poems, I followed the order in which the Dutch poems appear in the different collections.

Peeters' work has been published in many international journals and has been translated for festivals too, but this is the first collection of Peeters' work to appear in English.

Peeters is a poet who found her voice early, and her work, which continues to develop in new directions, has its own very distinctive flavour. I hope this book gives the reader a sense of the breadth and depth of this poet's work.

Judith Wilkinson

Enough about Love for Today

1999

'SHALL I WALK WITH YOU SOME OF THE WAY?'

Why not. You may walk with me as far as the traffic lights
or as far as the very next underpass.
As far as the third street on the right,
as far as the entrance to the park.
As far as the hospital, as far as beyond
the hospital, right up to my front door.

You may walk with me as far as inside my room,
as far as a glass of something or other,
as far as when I've brushed my teeth
or when the first morning light
falls across the chair with the clothes.

As far as when the construction workers start their day,
as far as when school opens,
the civil servants have their break,
the shops close
or as far as the departure of the last slow train.

As far as after waking up but before breakfast,
as far as after breakfast but before lunch,
as far as after lunch but before supper
you may walk with me.

WALKING A TIGHTROPE

Always in search of a navel string,
since the first one no longer exists,
I balance on the flimsy thread
between glances, until the moment
when I you
and you I once more.

Connected again suddenly
we are suspended above the ground.
With no more distance between us,
I feel the cosmos would easily
fit into one hand.

Your words taste like sweets.
You conjure kisses from your pockets.
I swallow them, steal them, store them
for later.

When the tightrope
twists in mid-air
into a snare,
I fall.

YOU'RE NO LONGER SMALL ENOUGH

You're no longer small enough
to disappear into yourself.
A thousand curtains can't conceal
the scope of you.

Your step drives footprints into the floor.
Your hand sets whirlwinds free.
Your voice cuts to the core.

If you ever wither to a wisp,
sink, horizontal, or inside an urn,
beneath the prints your foot pressed
in the ground

or if your ashes scatter above the sea,
caught up in all the whirlwinds
your hand had set free,

if your voice is given a say
by being silent, the wind
appears to spell your name,

you'll still be too large to disappear
to that distant, distant place
where you once were.

I lie waiting in the white
between the lines between the
words between the sentences,
I hear nothing but the quiet purring
of the monitor, my pen
no longer scratching. I am
the white the wait the view
in the black. Look for me softly
with fingers of sight.

The trapeze artist falls.
His foot abandoned him.
Short-sightedness of his senses,
a blind moment's mistake.

Many-headed, the audience squints
in unanimous disappointment;
he'd seemed so far above them.

He isn't scared. The earth
catches him. In her stony hands
he's cradled back into the ring.

> *El mar, la mar*
> *¿Por qué me trajiste acá? a la ciudad*
> – Rafael Alberti

The sea, the sea, the seaaaaaa
that's still there too.
My father didn't take me
there. My mother
didn't let me play on the beach.
In summer I'd stay behind
in the city, where the sand
was nothing but streets.

The little ships had wheels. The road
was always flat. I kept going under
in the waves of iron on the roof
with my winged fish.

I'd scoop tinned food into my bucket
with the shell of my hand.
I spent my days
finding lots of pebbles.

I built, built fair and square
my castles
in the air.

DATE

He didn't show up.
Perhaps he fell ill or was hit
by a tram, perhaps someone else
spoke to him. Perhaps he forgot his watch
or the watch forgot to tell him the right time.
Perhaps his car wouldn't start
or it broke down half way.
Perhaps he got a phone call when he was about to set off,
telling him he had to go to a cremation
or that his mother had died.
Perhaps he ran into an old acquaintance.
Perhaps he had a row at work
or he got fired and buried his head
under a pillow.
Perhaps the bridge was up, and the next one too.
Perhaps the traffic light got stuck on red.
Perhaps the cashpoint swallowed his card
or he discovered, on his way to me, that he'd forgotten his wallet.
Perhaps he lost his glasses
or couldn't stop reading
or wanted to see the end of a TV programme
or the lock on his front door failed,
he couldn't find his keys anywhere
and suddenly his dog threw up.
Perhaps his mobile battery had gone flat,
he couldn't find the restaurant
or he's waiting for me somewhere else.
Perhaps—the last inconceivable
and unforeseen possibility—
he no longer loves me.

TWONESS

I don't want to hang on your lips,
I don't want to take cover in the shell of your ear
and get lost in the jungle of your hair

or ski from the bridge of your nose, drink coffee
in the shelter of your lashes
and paddle in your blue eyes.

I don't even want to dance on your cheeks, dive
from your tongue and land on your teeth
or wade through your saliva.

But let your wrinkles be the paths
on which I set out, always together,
and walk to the end of my own life.

For years now you've occupied
every room in my head.
I just can't seem to
get rid of you.

I've put other names
in, but none
sticks
the way yours does.

I run into it in the
brand of clothes I buy,
you play a part in every
film I see

and in the street I hear your name
being called out so often
that I wonder how it's possible
that you're unique
and yet so current.

I don't believe you act
in films and you certainly
don't live in my head.
I wish you did. You live

somewhere in a seaside cottage,
where you gaze out of the window.
You're waiting. For me. But
you've forgotten my name.

A Suitcase Full of Sea Air

2003

LAST NIGHT I RAN INTO MY PARENTS

Last night I ran into my parents,
two pale shadows inclining towards
each other in the glow of a street light.

Judging by their happiness I hadn't yet
been born. They were young and very much in love.
A great sadness weighed me down,
knowing how the story would unfold.

He whispered something and she laughed out loud.
He roared with laughter as he still often does.
Briefly we exchanged civilities
and then we went our separate ways.

'We'll meet again,' I called out after them,
'you'll see, our paths will cross.' They didn't speak.
Arm in arm they turned the corner of the street.

A SOFT STONE

I am the stumbling stone my parents decided
to stumble over only once, so I'm alone.

I am the pebble-stone of contention in the gravel
at the front door of their cardboard façade,
I commemorate—as a memorial stone—
the end of what was once a home,

I am the gravestone of a person without surname,
the rock that Sisyphus was condemned to by the gods,
the millstone round the cripple's neck.

I carve myself into a thousand toes,
to stub them endlessly on the slightest things.
I am a soft stone from which no shoot springs.

THE SAME SEA

I alone know both my parents:
preferring not to err repeatedly,
they bathed just once in the same sea.

Since then their lives have gone their separate ways,
like coasts along a sea I navigate,
only to founder again out of their sight.
Somewhere in the distance lies another fate.

Once on dry land, will I, as their daughter,
fail to create a haven for myself,
made restless by the changing tides,
their troubled waters?

GOD HELP US THAT FATHER OF MINE

God help us that father of mine was always first
into the breach where injustice was concerned.
He was a fellow traveller, co-mover
on the waves of history, he chronicled them
with a steady hand, bulletlessly staunch,
he braved misty cities in remote places,
parted with more than the shirt off his back,
but less than the skirt that my mother pulled up
to give birth to me.

Goddamn it that father of mine I was so proud of
that I wanted to follow him,
a fellow babe in arms;
even on his knee I travelled upsy-daisy
on a camel through the desert with the caravan
far away from her who years later still lay
moaning in the aftermath in her bedroom
where no wink of sleep no chink of daylight was allowed,
no fresh air, no foreign country
and no father's face to make her wilt even more
than on the day I spilt out of her.

But my father, ay ay compañero, was in Chile,
Nicaragua, on a steamer across the ocean,
in the slammer in Bolivia with beard, knife and hat
busy finding the world too small for himself
while she raised a whole new life on her own.

My footprints melt in snow.
They take on the shape of some unintended animal
before suddenly vanishing halfway.

THE DIAMOND

The train set itself in motion
she kept her eyes closed
blindly searched for her handkerchief
with her left hand

on the other a ring sparkled
with the small diamond that I prised out
because her fingers so soft
and the diamond so hard, because
our fingers were entwined
and mine went everywhere

I knew that I couldn't yet know
that's why I so loved
or perhaps why she let me
have things my way
so sadly often.

She rang the bell. A drawn-out scream
filled the room in which I didn't move.

She rang and rang that bell; I bowed my head.
Then silence fell. I heard the dripping

of the tap. The neighbours' mellow music swelled
to a crescendo. Alone I stayed there with the moon,

that great big eye, the pupil in the universe's iris,
that followed everything since it was cold

enough to bear what it confronted.
To her I'd been that far moon at the window.

Unapproachable to me the street below.
Her gaze a question. I was what she wanted.

THE GREAT TREK

I saw the neighbours opposite one morning
packing their cases with sea air.
My caravan of playmates became the tail
of their kite, waving from the window of their car,
snagging briefly on a balcony
before they turned the corner.

They set out for the City of Sandcastles,
a stone's throw away from Amsterdam, said the stay-at-homes,
a world away from Amsterdam, said they
who were headed for the fresh sea breeze, a flight
that changes parents into pioneers.

Not mine. Somewhere halfway, the sun
struck its shadow into the aquarium of our apartment
where I was pressed against the glass, growing ever paler
as my gaze followed their disappearance
until they'd turned the corner of my memory.

On the coast, my mother later said, they too were torn apart.
Although they did live there, for a little while,
in airy bunkers with open windows.

MEMORY OF AN UNFINISHED MOMENT

An intermediate stage and yet the end of the world,
an interval to breathe in the blustery wind,
a moment to invent silence,
a horizon for the distant gaze to settle on.

My sandcastle was never engulfed by the sea
in the eternity of July
to the sound of screeching gulls.

The shrimps I caught still splash about in my pail
and my mother goes on
sunning herself
with a broad smile on her face.

Her legs of oil
on my fingers,
mayonnaise
that I wipe off on this page.

The ship rises up like Noah's Ark—
but one that lets everybody in.
We embark for a certain destination.

THE SEA IS AN ETERNAL MURMURER

With a faint roar the sea gathers force,
announces itself to the beach,
only to eat its words again
and return to a profound nothingness,
the bottomless depths of loss.

Sometimes it raises its voice,
tosses itself at our feet,
stirs up our restlessness,
awakens our fears, rushes back again
with the same roar that announced its arrival.
Every time it takes back its secrets
and leaves us behind without them.

At night its vast plain stretches
sky-wide in a macabre darkness
that has lost its tongue but stares at us
all the more wide-eyed. We propose a toast again and again.
There's nothing else we can do.
We're not built to handle so much silence.

IN THEIR SHADOW

It is the fate of generations
to be separated, time and again,
and to prize open different worlds
all on this one and only earth.

The future has no room for the elderly,
the distant past accommodates no minors
and the rest no dead people.
They live in one another's shadow.

After the day has risen
they go on sleeping
in chambers that cut across our walls
while we talk slap through them.

A LAST SALUTE

Gentlemen, highly respected Admirals of the Fleet, Vice-Admirals,
Rear Admirals, you have done history
a service but you've been dismissed by the present.

Dear Commodores,
captains and commanders,
however high your standing once was,
your class is now superfluous.

Esteemed lieutenants and sub-lieutenants
and highly regarded midshipmen,
your honour has proved mortal, your uniforms are moth-eaten.

All you can do now is march through eternity,
salute the clouds,
elevate yourselves to statues
of an unshakeable character.

The All Saints' Flood has receded.
The sea, though not convinced,
has been contained by the embankment
and now toes the line
drawn by man.

The shipworm, termite of the ocean,
renowned underminer of dikes,
hit rock bottom
at Den Helder's unyielding sea wall.

Big guns
drove the English back.

Today only the navy
knocks at the gate of your abandoned breastworks,
blowing its own trumpet.

IF EVER

If ever your touch should no longer disturb me
or only annoy me or leave me cold, if ever
the days should close in again, in an endless
dry enumeration
without apotheosis if death
should mingle with us and sit at our table
joylessly, with nothing but the tedious
chatter of our forks,

if ever your blood should no longer be mine
or I drink it and there's more in the room
than your presence while you're with me,
if ever wallpaper and hat-rack with your coat on it
should leave me indifferent
and the street lies resigned at our feet,

then I'll ask you to come with me
in a small coffin under a tree where we once,
or to burn and be tossed in the water
that we set out on once, to go back to the places
in the photo album and even the photo album
with everything still in it and even our house, the kids
if we have them then, the whole earth
we'll have to bury together, if ever

YOUR BODY

Your body yes your body
your hairy shameless body
your shimmering white body
your sprawling stretched out body

that stares at me with caverns and crannies
with tufts and curls and plumpness
or skulks under sheets and weavings
or bulges out of suits and trappings

it's always your body your body
your lazily seductive body
your sinuous tapering body
your invisible arousing body

your shamelessly spreading body
your noisily coming body
your turning-towards-me body
your turning-away-from-me body

your never-strange-to-me body
your never-unknown-to-me body
your never-unloved-by-me body
your ever-present body

A FOREGONE CONCLUSION

It was fate brought us together
and that was nice

whether it will drive us apart again
is the question

it could easily have kept us to itself
and made us unhappy.

But here we are:
still together and we wonder but daren't

assume: for how long
has fate touched the two of us simultaneously

and cajoled us into
living in the softness of its claws?

It was fate, a foregone conclusion,
that led to improbably violent shivers of desire.

NOTE

Dearest, I had to hurt you
because writing doesn't go with happiness.
So you had to break.
But know this: it is the gentlest kind of breaking,
a written one,
being nothing more than the thoughts
of something as harmless
as a poet.

ILLUSION

This morning while I wasn't yet awake
and not asleep either, doom crept in
on cloven socks, nestled invisibly
against me and spoke my name, a whisper—
not wanting to wake me.

Without opening my eyes I saw him
look at me, though his eyes too were shut.
He stroked the pillow, he mistook it for my lips
and it kissed him back the way I would have kissed.
We embraced in the assumption of each other.

GOODBYE

At the bus stop I kissed the air
around your cheek and pushed you away from me,
against the wall, to punish you
for your complaining.

From their doorsteps neighbours stared.
Others peered through net curtains,
while we stood there.

The bus in which I'd meant to sit and cry
went by and then went by again.
And when the next one came
I still didn't dare get in.

Once again I stayed behind,
to take shelter from
what I had done
to you, you to me.

HOLLAND'S DELUGE

In penury the ancients built this land
to what it is today: enclosure dam and airport rose

from the sea and pavestones from the streets,
the youth are jigging underground,

mosques hum, bells toll for a distant
god to enter still

but in these lowlands the rain beats against
rattling attic windows

and beneath them the sad monotonous fumbling
in a bed, the predictable moaning:

harder, faster, deeper boy,
until the bedposts break,

until the posts break and the dikes burst,
flooding the polders from their thighs.

ECCE HOMO

Perhaps he's the illegitimate crossbreed of a devil
and an angel, with one foot on the ground
and his arms in the clouds, perhaps he invented
pornography and is now sleeping a downy sleep.

Perhaps God created him in a fit of self-mockery
on a forgotten ninth day and he didn't smile
because he saw that it was good, but because it was typical
and, for an ambivalent God, showed certainty of touch.

Perhaps he breathes solace into our final breath
and prophesies eternal love, while yawning
with the benevolently cruel and ever-present smile
of an inverted Mona Lisa hovering round his mouth.

He may be found snorkeling in some egocentric sea or other,
or breathing in forest air, torturing cats to death, writing chronicles
full of fairytales, prompting presidents or inhaling gunsmoke
and microbes.

Perhaps he's the best that could be made of him:
born out of an ambitious accident and despite evolution's
aftercare still incomplete and above all
mortal.

LAMENT OF THE SLEEPLESS SLEEPING BEAUTY

Silence has fallen in the palace, where all the ladies-in-waiting
    are asleep,
where my father the clement king has laid himself down to rest.
The guard is snoring in front of the high gate
but his ears remain alert and are pricked up
for any sound other than his own snoring.
The footmen are in their box beds.
The marquises are slumped around the beer tap.
Even the mice are asleep and the cats too.
The bats and the spiders.
The whole place is fast asleep.
Only Sleeping Beauty is still awake.
The peonies in the garden are asleep.
The maze is utterly deserted.
In the moat the ducks are asleep.
On the battlements the pigeons.
The bell-ringer is asleep with the bell-rope in his hands.
The weathervane sleeps in the wind that is asleep too,
although it hasn't died down.
The clouds have tucked themselves
into a blanket of darkness.
But the princess still briefly roams the corridors.
The horses are asleep on their feet.
The chickens sleep on one leg with their beaks hidden in their
    feathers.
The cannons are also asleep, and the gunpowder and the
    hunting rifles.
The seamstresses have slipped into a deep sleep in their sewing
    room.
The carpenters have tumbled off the chairs they had made.
In the hands of the baker the bread is growing stale.
The farmers are lying stretched out on their land,
hidden beneath the crops they were harvesting.

The sparrows are asleep, as are the parakeets and the crows.
The barber's customers are sleeping in their freshly trimmed beards.
The ghosts are asleep in the attic and in the cellar the rats are asleep.
Only the princess is unable to fall asleep any time this century.

LAMENT OF THOSE WHO LISTEN TO WAR REPORTS

Dust raised the days of the flesh,
flesh turned to dust.
In the interim rooms remained empty,
spring came, birds flew,
bombs were hatched.

We spilt Coca-Cola on newspapers all summer long,
let the voice on the radio rattle on.
Music swiftly wiped out every news flash
and on my face lay your hand.
Bombs didn't fall here
another bottle of Coke toppled over.

Your mouth went in search of the glass.
The switch dimmed the radio voice.
The dead floated away in the Coca-Cola and
people were getting raped. We were busy loving.
As if that were possible.

Runner of Light

2008

IN THE DESERT

I was considered too impudent
an eternity ago
banished to the desert
and here

—do you see that Arabian steed
that horse of iron wire
that bellowing Guernica?
That's me.

By the time the sand
that flies up from under my feet
and blinds you
as I pass
drifts down before your eyes,
I'll be gone.

The dromedary unfolds itself
vertebra by vertebra
rises in jolts to its feet and undulates
clunkily from sight.

A black sun
rises above my eye.
This blurred lens seems to ensure
that everything's a mirage.

Stiffly nothing stretches
fully yet but lingers before the furthest
point is reached a beat or two behind
until the caravan of limbs
is ready to accept the journey.

What is heard has been banished from the ear,
roams the furthest passageways of the vault
and flows out in echoes of memory.

There it soars like a bird, too high
to hear the beating of the wings
and yet a whirling sound
and the protesting wind
still strike a chord, somewhere.

Then the sense of touch grows numb
as if the living had become the dead,
even this child I caress
and place beside a stump
that casts no hint of shadow.

As far as the eye stretches—
a child, a cry and nothing but this wilderness.

EXILE

They banished me with the best of intentions,
asserted: with divine approval
we planted you here in our home.
Your confinement gave occasion
to so much yearliness after the event
but still no reason
to allow you into our deepest lives.

We are alone, as self-contained as one half
that has never known the other.
Immediately after halving the husk grew back
around our flesh.
We are complete, so in what sense do you accompany us?

You made us party
to good intentions
an indefinable abundance
progeny.

But the very fact that you—so long
after that particular one-offness
on which all this relies—continue to exist,
is not enough. Was it a single glance?
Some random word? How did you persuade yourself
that you should be accepted, to our dying day,
without further ceremony,
with a gesture that was its own prompter?

Go away.

IN THE NAME

Hagar is my name
which stands for outcast or stranger
although it's never certain what my name is.

Spiralling in the smoke of your cigarette
are all the shapes you never took, identities nonetheless yours,
they cast their shadows
on the ceiling and on walls,
the talents you never brought to light.

That veil of smoke is also
a succession of shoulders
of all the ancestors who passed themselves on
to you. You were burdened
with their gift.

We bring out a toast, at table,
to everything that escapes us. Smoke envelops us
completely. Now the world has been smothered.

Smoke, that is to say, hands
that carry you to heights
from which nearly everything is bearable.
Just look at me:
there are many shades of Hagar.

Such as Ayaan
daughter of Hirsi—
known as the son of Magan, almost certainly a child of Isse
most probably the son of Guleid
in all conceivable likelihood the son of Ali
almost undoubtedly the son of Wai'ays
who was the son of Muhammed, at least according to tradition,
of Ali, of Umar,

a Darod, a Majeerteen,
an Osman Mahamud, a Magan
of the Osman line—
who has now been driven away.

To the earliest evolution of ovulation
to tribes and plains
camps and lineages, lords and clans
to the limit we lead back.

All those stubborn Reubenites—a single patriarch's progeny
elbowing for survival—
such as Hanochites, Palluites, Hezronites
Carmites, or Nemuelites, Jaminites, Jachinites, Zarhites
barely distinguishable from one another.
Or Dathan and Abiram, Shaulites; the families of Simeonites
who in their turn were Israelites.

Shelanites, Pharzites, Zarhites, Hamulites
Tolaites, Punites, Jashubites, Shimronites
Shemidaites, Hepherites—different,
though perhaps not obviously so,
from Shutalhites, Bachrites, Tahanites, Eranites.

Don't forget the Zephonites, Haggites, Shunites, Oznites—the
    unstoppable.
The Erites, Arodites and Arelites—the impetuous.
Machirites, Gileadites, Jeezerites, Helekites
(they crawled out of nooks and crannies).

Belaites, Ashbelites, Ahiramites, Shuphamites,
to the outsider
like peas in a pod,
the Jimnites, the Jesuites, Beriites,
headstrong in their own unique way
as were the Gershonites, Kohathites, Merarites
Libnites, Hebronites, Mahlites.

Not even including the descendants of Ishmael
named after their parentage
after their hamlets and their encampments
twelve princes according to their tribes.

And they lived from Havilah to Shur
east of Egypt
on the way to Assyria.

He kept his word.
Father Abraham's progeny was vast.

Ites
isms
egos.

That's more or less how the story went.

REASSURING

Father Abraham, primordial patriarch,
didn't lose any sleep over death;
the hereafter is a bit like sleep-tight
when you stay the night at a friend's house,
but without returning home.

He dreamt up descendants for himself
something more abiding than one day's incidence of light
the angles of descent fathoms deep, telescopically remote
when lenses are adjusted to it
diaphragms tightened
like thumbscrews of the moment.

The moment eludes the viewer, is thinner
than a thumb and nimbler than Tom Thumb
but as for the vast hereafter, he adjusted
his prospect until it fitted.

BROKEN

Sarah, his spouse for centuries,
stood on her toes
to get his attention,
but as soon as she got it, she let it slip
because he saw her. This led to broken pieces
to be picked up one by one,
which demanded attention and led
to her asking for yet more attention.

You might cut yourself on the pieces.
Should you overlook one,
things would never be the same again.

They each grabbed some glue and joined
themselves together. As in the old days.

In the cups of their cavities
they formed
an incomplete but unbreakable whole.

SHE KNEW

He who sees me, sees other women too
he who doesn't see other women, doesn't see me either
he who loves with the passion of surrender
surrenders to love that lies hidden in the passion of surrender
he who forgets himself in the full emptiness of a vagina
knows himself forgotten in the finite oblivion of the vagina
he is the drowning man who drags himself ashore in the hands
    of a woman
he is the drowning man who is dragged ashore by a woman's hands
naked as an infant at the mercy of her whom fate gave him as a
    mother
that's how he lies in the arms of a woman to whom fate gave
    him as a lover
he loves all women in this one woman
and without their likeness she too disappears
he loves the ghosts and shadows that coincide
with the slender thighs and hips out of which he moulds his
most beloved image
from beyond his field of vision she walks towards him
he sees her only when he closes his eyes
when his dreams come tumbling in she tumbles into his arms
in their slumber the slow breathing of bodies that have become one
beneath the veil of the bed that keeps her covered she is all names
beneath the veil of the bed that keeps them covered
he sleeps with her and with all of them
he has to kill himself to keep her and her alone
once he was dead he couldn't love her any more.

HOW I SOUNDED

You have a sweet little gob
especially when you purse your lips
exchange kisses with the air
and talk frothy claptrap.

Between your teeth
your daft little tongue
the rebellious nib
that funny uvula of yours.

All that mumbling and mumbo jumbo,
I just can't get enough of it.
I don't find better nonsense in books.
As soon as it sinks in you sing it free again.

Come and lie next to me a bit longer
and do that again, that thing with your lips.
There's absolutely nothing else I need.

MISERABLE

How he, love-sick,
lay in bed and couldn't get to sleep
because He was whispering in his ear:
I'm still here, don't kid yourself.
You won't get rid of me.

In his tossing and turning
He turned along with him.
All that time He never let go
of his hand and He kept stroking
his clammy forehead. It was only
when he got up to meet Him
that He fell away.

Like scales, like ashes.
Then he stepped across them
put on his coat
closed the door behind him—
but left it just ajar.

THE DOOR AJAR

offered a glimpse
of the bedroom where Sarah
basked in her expansive afternoon,
toying with all her hours
like an infant with its toes,
pointing at the seconds like a seconds-hand
and claiming every second he was hers.

She lacked a sense of urgency
and if she did have an internal clock
its ticking didn't penetrate.
It was too late. Suddenly, it dawned on her:

I've slept right through the mother
I did not become, the one who got up
in the dead of night, to nurse her child.

She knows I wasn't ripe for it yet
I, her older sister, her mistress,
always a step behind her, less tried and tested
in rolling over from one side to another.
Even time itself didn't wake me.

Right up to the moment when dawn irons away
the last remnants of night, she watches
over everything, even over
my never having become the person she is, and she
understands it better than I do and is at peace with it.

The rot is setting in, there are marauders about.
Abraham has been nagging for so long.
He simply must have progeny, he must.
Even if it isn't mine.

Perhaps our maid from Egypt.
I see him leering at her, the bastard,
when she sweeps the floors under his feet
and he, while pretending to read,
glances at her from under his paper—

a glance he never casts at me any more.
He calls her Venus,
of all things, though her name is Hagar.

It seems to me it's not such a crazy idea
if, for this special occasion,
he should have her,
then we will keep the child
and dump her in the Sahara during our holiday.

I've broached the subject with him. He sees a loophole
there, he says, laughs. And she? She doesn't speak
our language yet so we can't ask her anything.
Nor will she know the way to the police
once he has raped her. So that's
all right. He may as well do it tonight.

PLACE OF ANTICIPATION

The house of the exile
is a house with doors
that open and close in both directions
so that arrival and departure
take place in a single flowing movement
as with a revolving door
in the centre of which the exile
waits to be shut in.

The house is not a dwelling place
but a place of anticipation.
All the rooms are waiting rooms.

The sofa in the sitting room
offers only a brief respite
from pacing up and down.

The literature in the bookcases
is made up of forms
and contains no poetry
only ordinances

As final as the orders are
so indefinite are the days.

The windows are windows
through which a landscape can be traced
that will soon no longer be visible
and in which the vista
of origin betrays itself.

When the exile leaves his house
he follows the signs that say 'exit',
which he'll encounter wherever he arrives.

WHAT FOLLOWED

All that multiplicity of future conflict
surfeit of discord and division
being sown like the grain on earth
with deportees and exiles as the offshoots
all those on the run for their convictions
those placed behind windows against their will
those stolen, traded or driven away
germinating as that same grain
as countless as the stars
nameless in number
and without name.

AN EXAMPLE

Like the man who knows
he's losing.
It started with one humiliating experience
whereupon matters went downhill.

Numerous times he married unhappily.
His children failed in the possibilities
that hadn't been offered to him.

He looks at his hands.
Somewhere they have missed their hold.
He tries to remember when that was

folds them in his lap
and so assumes the opposite posture
to that of a person reaching out

or perhaps he is counting his fingers
without anyone noticing.

ADVICE—NO STRINGS ATTACHED

Sometimes a pause is enough.
Before you answer, during a conversation,
count to ten on your fingers
but without anyone noticing;
this is how long the suggestion of listening takes.

Keep looking the person opposite you in the eye.
Avoid staring by nodding now and then
(follow the movement of the chin).

Be gracious when you arrive
and when you're about to go home.
Leave a token of your appreciation.

EN ROUTE

The exile uses many means of transport
to dispatch himself:

his own two feet, on sandals made of car tyres,
the iron horse, the golden coach,
the silver rainbow bird, the bronze steam locomotive—
outdated, verdigris-coated—
hidden in the landscape.

The camouflage of the exile
is his passport, with inside a photo
that almost equals him.

RULES OF THE GAME

When one exile runs into another
they play poker, but not for money.

The winner is given
a prophecy as reward.

Because it's only a game
the loser gets new chances.

EVEN THE WIND HAS AN OPINION

The wind thinks
it's seen just about enough
of all this living on air
and asks the earth for help
but the earth refuses.

It already belongs, says the earth,
to someone or other
whereas the wind is still free.

The wind is free, the wind answers,
because it has nothing to offer.

THE SAYING GOES

Just as a Roman army, after a defeat,
accepted the journey back
so, after every loss, a journey back is possible.
Accept it.

Don't accept the loss
but the journey back that follows it
all the way into your own entrenchment,
the body's armour

all the way to where you were
before the loss followed
and choose something else.

A road to Rome.

HAGAR'S AMBITIONS

Let me be one of the decadents and drink with the men.
Let me follow you, Baudelaire, Whitman, Campos
all the great self-believing conquerors
all those who ride on the backs of dangerous animals
all those who raise their voices without shame
let me be one of you with blusher on my cheeks
and carefully eye-lined glance.
Cheers!

You are the inventors of self-conscious debauchery,
proud degenerates who see their dissolution as an ascent into heaven.
Let me, with hair gathered up and a necktie,
waistcoat, trousers, shirt, and breasts on my chest
and a few locks in my neck that wave about with every breeze,
raise a toast to our like-mindedness.
To our health!

Lift me onto the backs of your elephants and let me ride with
    you into the wilderness.
Let me put on these grubby trousers and follow you, you vagabonds.
I want to knock around with the great men.
I want to join the mighty fathers on their travels.
Let them show me the world that lies at my small feet.
Open up the continents to me, drive my elephants, together
    with the slaves,
along the path carved through the jungle,
let the labourers look up to me
and let me, whose nails are painted red, though dirt-rimmed
    from scratching,
be one of those labourers whom I strike across his back
while shouting with the voice of the master:
Santé!

My boots will stamp through puddles of rainwater
that has fallen equally for everyone—for what does the rain care?
And I want to chronicle the world's tales of shame

only to erase them again immediately and rewrite them
for I want to cry like a woman for all the pain ever suffered
and cradle children against my tender breast
during one of the meetings of your club, clan, regiment, society
  or committee

and I will reserve the right to reject proposals
yes, to reject you, regardless of how it will hurt or offend you.
I don't love out of pity.
Make me a partner in your card games,
you bunch of brigands and pirates. Don't leave me screaming
  on the sidelines
or fearful of vermin that creep over the earth and in my hair.
I'm all set to join in the hunt, the romps, the tournaments.
Cheers! Cheers! Cheers!

Fathers of the world, take pity.
Make an exception, just this once, so you can set a precedent
that will be binding, for evermore,
by allowing me access to all the world's kingdoms and domains
that have been taboo for me since time immemorial
because it suited those in charge of these crown properties.

Let me squander the cheques you have written.
All the things that bear your mark
all the inventions you have patented
let me handle them sensuously
toss them round my shoulders casually
distribute them to children
feed the hungry sparrows
let me play Santa Claus with them
let me manage them nonchalantly
and make irresponsible purchases with them
but entrust them to me nevertheless.

I want the key to the forbidden chamber
the code to the computer, access to systems
the password to profitable domains.
Let me waft my fans and hurl my lassoes

all in one single motion.
To compensate for your strength, leave me my weapons
and essential equipment.
Hand the floor over to me and don't immediately interrupt me.
Risk talking to me at parties
without the promise of a voluptuous night.

I will break off the heels of my stilettos.
I refuse to go on stumbling across the pavestones
unless they are the tiles that lead to my own palaces,
and whatever limits my freedom of movement,
renders me invisible or shuts me out,
I shall cast off, or cast before the feet
of him who provoked me, before I trample it underfoot.
And if you ask me to strip off as many clothes as possible
I shall order you to lead the way
and leave it at that.

Fruition

2011

MY GRANDMOTHER WAS A FRONT SOLDIER

In my grandmother's village
the women came to fruition once a year
developed new shoots bore fruit
there was blossoming round the clock
bloodiness from the dead, the miscarried
the misshapen and the ordinary viable ones.

In the village a front mentality
reigned;
the women were soldiers
pitted against the dominant majority
of the dissenters
approaching from all sides.

Armed with pregnancy
they obeyed submissively
but when the viable foetuses
had matured and grown up
and had left the battle field
it wasn't the emperor who was checkmated
but the mother who had no heaven
to rely on, nor a life
to look back on.

Just as the father's leather belt
and the teacher's ruler
beat the hand of the disobedient
so the church bell beat out its calling
to the medieval rhythm of sowing
and mowing and harvesting
whereupon the pastor would arrive at the door
to inspect the armour of pregnancy
and every year he'd check the belly's curvature
of the pregnancy-armed front soldier and serf
my grandmother was.

The toll of a bell
is like a blow to the face
of the man who listens to the tolling
and bends until he's on his knees
in the corn in the field
that wouldn't grow otherwise.

THE GRANDMOTHER AND THE PRINCE

She carried crooked buckets to the sea
when she was seven years old

emptied them and
the horizon was crooked
the land was crooked
and the man who administered justice
wore a crooked beard.

She bore thirteen children
with flat feet on a flat earth
who played hopscotch, hopping oddly
on the odd numbers chalk-scrawled on the pavement.

In the evenings she'd call them to a table
whose corners were missing
and there wasn't much talk.

She scrimped and saved
and went without,
her belly bloated until she gave birth.

The day before her funeral
the mausoleum of a reprobate prince
was on TV, with a funeral procession
in every respect symmetrical:

fighter planes flew over in uniform loops,
leaving a perfectly straight space above the coffin.
The funeral was a delirious parade.

Here she lies in state:
her body speaks for itself.

GOD'S FLOSSERS

As thin as the thread was she
who, with a twisting motion, strung
life and death between his lips,
so thin that she slipped past his teeth
and lived off the loosened remnants.
This was her work, day in day out,
until his mouth was empty.
Then he ate her and others
were allowed to floss his gold teeth.
This was their work, day in day out,
until his mouth was empty.

MATRIARCH

Coarse hands lie on her chest.
Her cheekbones prominent and broad.
Her gaze has explored endless horizons,
her fingers kneaded men's skins.
She's a cheerful woman at the change of life.

Her hips are a ship's deck, vast,
her bosom the universal firmament,
with all that lies hidden beneath.
Terraces and deserts found a place in her belly,
she wears shawls of coloured silk.

Here she comes to our table.
She'll be chased off again.
She raises her hand to read palms,
to knead skin or massage toes
for a few miserable centavos, forints or kopeks.

IN THE MUSEUM

What map do we set our course by from here?
The Italian portolan,
so readily available in the museum?
It saw every ocean it depicts.
It hung in a ship, as the hole in its hide testifies.
Prehistoric drawing pins got their hooks into it.

Thanks to it, slaves were traded,
silk worms found and costly plans hatched.
It sailed round Scylla and Charybdis,
the Cyclops-eyed cliff
and circumvented the infinite whirlpool.
Everywhere it came ashore safely.

Now it hangs here smugly behind glass.
Does it want to show me the way again?
Of course. Naturally. With love.
But that no longer exists, I gather.

THE VAGUE RUMOUR

I knew about you before I knew about you;
age-old love lyrics had broadcast your existence,
ambassadors in the form of books had run ahead of you,
announcing your arrival.

I'd seen in films how a kiss is executed
and learned, from other films, about reproduction.
It wasn't much; my knowledge limited,
but it was enough to make me long for you.

And yet you only partly corresponded
to what little I had gathered about love.
I found you and I kept searching for you.
We were together but hardly one.

We shelved the end of our inseparableness
by hugging each other tightly.
And it stopped us from running
until we ran from stopping ourselves from running.
And love became a vague rumour once again.

DEBUT

The first night that she spent awake
in a barn with him—
the one she denied her first kiss—
she still remembers after many nights of waking.

She'd stayed there motionless, eyes shut,
not sure how to begin
what neither of them had
ever done before.

Slowly the light from outside
had pushed its way in through the window
and with it her reason for lingering
had vanished to an elsewhere
beyond her reach, she realises, even today.

AFTER HANS ANDREUS

Take yourself far away from me
take yourself out of my sight
take every message you sent me
take yourself away, take yourself away.

Hurry away from me
be farther away than you are
allow distance to grow between us
take yourself away, take yourself away.

Get lost, get lost in this
dull and dreadful blankness
remove yourself far and wide
leave me now that you hide.

THE ONE HE WAS LOOKING FOR

On every park bench
the woman he was looking for
became more ageless.
In the café her laugh
was the only one.

He walked up to benches,
sat at bars,
waited and listened,
gazed around him a little, spoke.

It was her
who was never the one.

THE ACCIDENT

There had been decline. There had been defeat.
There were words from the living later.
There was confusion. There was wistfulness.
There was an empty car at the side of the road.
There was a wrecked coupé in the valley.
There were disaster tourists, reporters,
camera folk. There were articles in the paper.
There were photos of the photographers. There was sand.
There had been no farewell, there had been no time for that.
And there was regret, though no one knew what about.
It seems I died last week.
I was hit by something unnamable,
when I crossed over, without looking, from me to you.

I RECOGNISE YOU

In the murky submarine struggle
of the sweatiest hour
in the darkness of the deepest chasm
in the crevices of our closed eyes
the hollows and the balls

in this between-sheets sublunary revolt
this between-poems overriding
white forgetting
this downy dissipation of fear and pain
this womb-mimicking darkness
in this wet and weary night
in which we kindle the fires of hell
the shadows mimicking our movements
in the flickering candlelight
where, together, we're one rider on horseback
this arm and this hand, decked out with a swift pen

in this interim in this oblivion
in this panting this grinding this moaning
this howling this going down howling
in this little death we die
but never forever
when you write poems
that I read

I recognise you

this little death we die together
so we can handle the big one alone.

FOR REMCO CAMPERT

When we grew tired
we went to sleep
and the cars drove in reverse.

Back in time the ceiling of our third-rate hotel
became a sky again
above the mattress that was the world.

It was too late to drink and fuck
and blather about birch trees
and their beauteous leaves.

Perhaps we lay there waiting
for a liberation,
perhaps we were reeling off a mini-revolution

or we were in hiding from the searchlights
of cars driving in reverse
who were oblivious to the fist-wide chink
clenched at them between the curtains,

but your fist on my shoulder was soft
and the room hung in the night like a moon.

I CARESSED YOUR POEMS

Blindly I let my fingers trace the lines,
caressing every masterstroke
and blushing at so much imperfection.

Once in a while I would be moved
as if I were naked before the paper,
the letters would filter through my torso
and a streak of cold pass through me.

Written backwards, my amazement
had been ready in me for centuries
and I reread with both my hands.

THE CALL I HEARD IN MYSELF

Hearing the sounds of a piano from a window—
not meant for me,
I just happened to become aware of them
as I walked past,
an audience for this chance occurrence
that was like an unintended gift,
a gift for me, for me alone—
I think of sounds I heard before,
walking past some other window once.
It was in Spain, Cordoba,
a street furtively wound its way up the hill
where we, on a terrace—
the chairs had been painted blue, as I suddenly
clearly remember—had something to eat
and it all seemed so self-evident,
the hot afternoon in Spain, the blue terrace,
the sounds of a piano from a window,
drifting, dying music.

MEMENTO OF THE FOLKINGESTRAAT IN GRONINGEN

Here our eyes study the house fronts
with their still quite recent
commemorative art, and we practise
not seeing any more, not ever being able
to look at it all any more, and when we shop
at one of the fifty-seven retailers
in this narrow street, tucked into the city
like a hiding-place, a secret cranny,

we relive the never shopping any more
at the baker's at the kosher horse butcher's,
we relive the never trading
here in this street of trade, this gateway
to the city and place of pilgrimage
where the synagogue has opened its doors again
and dwellings built of durable stone
in their simple presence
eternalise the fact that life here is a reliving
of the impermanence of life

that was cut short in this street that never stops
and in one of the numerous cafés,
here, where we are merry, we relive
the end of that merriness
for those who were deported in this street.

Poems for Wich

2012

BOAT

He painted a boat
and he named it after her
and on a straight wooden board
she sails
but not out of sight.
There's a white waving flag,
there's grey smoke coming from the chimney,
there's a small grey flag
on the after-hold
and there are two ladders
pointing towards the cargo.
I want to get on board!
I want to climb onto this wooden cargo boat
and sail and sail towards later.

THE LIGHT OF THE SEA

I want to conjure up the light of the sea,
just you try to explain that, he said,
and I try to explain it.

Look: the water doesn't stand there but radiates
outwards and the clouds rise up
from the blue of the water
and the clouds are the sea

only descended into water
and the light doesn't aim at anything,
it's simply there.

The light is simply there,
like the sea,
it's only the moment

that moves, but the light stays
the light stops still above the water
the light rises up out of the water

the sea is a big pan and the clouds
are the steam of the boiling water
and the clouds are white and underneath them
the light trembles

and there is still more light within the light
of the sea, more than you can see
and that's what I put into the painting
daubing on my very lightest paint
that still isn't white.

But that's how I picture it.
I try to explain
but the sea eludes
my explanation.

Precisely this
eternally elusive movement
is the sea.

Perhaps he saw a completely different light
in the sea.

Or perhaps he saw the sea
in a completely different light.

ABOUT DÉCORS

There stands the décor, beyond all praise
endlessly making time return
transcending transience
bringing the past back to life
turning dreams into reality
interpreting our longing
it stands straight-backed, strong-shouldered
it stretches its arms round the players
it casts its shadow across life

it is the bosom the womb of the dancers
it is the haven the cradle of the play
the ballerina measures her steps by it
and within the bounds of the theatre
in the light of the cardboard moon
we have the audience on one side
and the actors who transport us on the other

and in this hallowed conspiracy
this division of parts since time immemorial,
something magical happens:
the sounds and the figures, the intentions and the voices
the energy and the movements of everyone are held there,
beneath the dome of the décor, and infinitely magnified

The evening glows and stretches.
Outside, under a heavenless sky—
not counting the stars and the firmament—
the people leaving the theatre
talk about what they've seen
before dispersing, full of animation,
the evening engraved on their minds.

DÉCORS AND IN THE MEANTIME

And against the background of his décors
and alongside the parts played in his costumes
by character actors

for instance criss-cross on either side
of the dancers and their dance, and obliquely and
surreptitiously
and against the grain and in the meantime
there was his own life, flamboyant
and inescapable.

There were still many things
that eluded the hand of the artist

and sometimes he would sigh:
just as well.

STILL LIFE

Life grew quiet
ever more quiet
after a war an education
an innate discovered cherished and
evolved passion

after finding love and having children
the turbulence of a marriage
and divorce and the deaths of a sister a son
death

the unpredictable course
of success and loss and triumph
abandonment and retreat and recognition
and finding a new life
the warmth of love
the caress of paintbrushes

life grew more and more quiet
life grew more and more quiet

more and more peaceful more and more
intense, focused
on this one moment
this moment of this view
through these eyes

this single moment
of this momentary view
from a window
overlooking the sea

stillness descended
like this single light
of the sea

like the simplicity
of this painted sea.

This poem confirms
Remco Campert's saying
that poetry is an act of confirmation
that you're alive, that you're not alone.

This poem confirms the existence of people
who didn't live alone but were together
in every way they could be together.

Togetherness requires confirmation,
the confirmation of togetherness, and that's enough.
Just see: the repetition

of you in me and of me in you
and the acceptance
that it had to be like this.

Later I'll be just as old as you were when you went.
Old age will clamber onto me then
and I'll carry it the way you did.
It advances like cold from the ground in the morning,
first to my feet, later to my temples.

I'll think of you then, how you were old
and yet not old, but endlessly yourself.
Did you know that time, too, is a décor,
a costume you can cast off?

NOTES

'Runner of Light', p. 41: the poems in this section were loosely inspired by the biblical story of Hagar.

'Fruition', p. 69: this section contains both recent work and work written in Peeters' late teens and early twenties. Peeters decided to mix old and new poems in the collection from which these poems were taken.

'After Hans Andreus', p. 79: Hans Andreus (1926–1977) is a well-known Dutch poet and children's book writer.

'For Remco Campert', p. 83: Remco Campert, born in 1929, is a celebrated Dutch poet and novelist whose work has been widely translated.

'Poems for Wich', p. 87: Harry Wich (1927–2002) was a well-known Dutch artist who designed sets and costumes for nearly all the major Dutch theatre companies. Later in his life he devoted himself exclusively to his painting. Hagar Peeters was commissioned to write *Poems for Wich* by Dorine de Vos, the widow of Harry Wich.

BIOGRAPHICAL NOTES

Hagar Peeters

Hagar Peeters, born in 1972, is one of Holland's best-known poets. Her first collection, *Genoeg Gedicht over de Liefde Vandaag* ('Enough said about love today'), gained her immediate recognition as a bold and distinctive new voice. Many of her subsequent collections—five to date—have been awarded prizes. In 2008 she was on the shortlist for Poet Laureate. She is also a critic, editor and columnist and has written a biography, *Gerrit de Stotteraar—Biografie van een Boef* ('Gerrit the stammerer—biography of a scoundrel', originally her M.A. thesis), in which she examines the life of this notorious Dutch burglar and escape artist in the context of the changes in the Dutch criminal justice system in the first decades after the Second World War. She has recently also turned to novel-writing and her first novel, Malva, was published in 2015.

Judith Wilkinson

Judith Wilkinson is a British poet and award-winning translator living in Groningen, the Netherlands. She has published many collections to date, including Toon Tellegen's *Raptors*, for which she won the Popescu Prize for European Poetry in Translation in 2011. In 2013 she won the Brockway Prize, a biennial prize for the translation of Dutch poetry. Two collections of her own poems, *Tightrope Dancer* (2010) and *Canyon Journey* (2016) were published by Shoestring Press. Some of her poems have been performed by the London dance-theatre company The Kosh.